Miniature Needlepoint Rugs for Dollhouses

Charted for Easy Use

Susan McBaine

Dover Publications, Inc., New York

Miniature Needlepoint Rugs for Dollhouses is
a new work, first published by Dover Publications,
Inc. in 1976.

International Standard Book Number: 0-486-23388-X
Library of Congress Catalog Card Number: 76-18406

Manufactured in the United States of America
Dover Publications, Inc.
31 East 2nd Street, Mineola, N.Y 11501

Introduction

The carpet designs in this collection are miniature adaptations of many different types of rugs, including Oriental, Persian, Early American, American Indian, modern and even animal skin. The color schemes given in the keys are more or less "authentic," but you may want to change the colors to suit your own tastes and needs.

Although the designs were originally charted for needlepoint, they can, of course, be used for many other crafts which use charted designs, such as counted cross-stitch, latch hooking, filet crochet, Fair Isle knitting and even mosaic work.

Whatever the project, it is a good idea to begin by carefully selecting the design. If you have never worked from a chart, begin with one of the fairly simple designs, such as the "Welcome Mat" or the "Octagonal Area Rug" on page 12, the "Modern Moroccan Rug" on page 34 or even the "Baluchi Prayer Rug" on page 27. As you become more proficient you can move on to some of the more complicated designs which involve many different changes of color, such as the "Medgedia Geordez Prayer Rug" on page 14 or the "Kurdish Kilim" on page 16. Study the pattern carefully to make certain that you know how the design works. Check the borders to see how they turn the corners. Analyze the repeating geometric motifs to see exactly where they overlap or join.

Most of the designs in this book are charted on 16-to-the-inch grids. (Details of some of the more intricate designs are show in 10-to-the-inch enlargements.) Each square represents one stitch to be taken on the canvas. You can render these designs on any size canvas that you wish, but to get a rug that will be close to the popular dollhouse scale of 1 inch equals 1 foot, use #18 canvas. The completed rug will be slightly smaller than the printed chart. All the rugs shown on the covers were done on #18 canvas with Persian wool used 1 ply.

If you wish to use these designs to make needlepoint purses, pillows, or belts, you will want to use a larger-mesh canvas, such as #10, #12 or #14. The very industrious embroiderer could make a full-sized area rug from some of these charts by needlepointing the design onto #3 or #5 rug canvas. To determine what size your finished project will be: count the number of squares on the chart, and divide this by the mesh size of the canvas you are using. For instance, if the chart measures 100 squares by 120 squares, a finished piece done on #10 canvas will be 10" x 12"; on #5 canvas the piece will be 20" x 24".

You will want to decide how to transfer the design onto the canvas before beginning. I enjoy working directly from the chart onto a blank canvas by counting off the corresponding number of squares and stitches. However, many people feel more comfortable following markings on the canvas, and draw some lines or even the entire pattern onto the canvas. If you decide to put any marks on your canvas, make absolutely certain that your medium is completely waterproof. Use either a non-soluble ink, acrylic paint thinned appropriately with water so as not to clog the holes in the canvas, or oil paint mixed with benzine or turpentine. Felt-tipped pens are also very handy, but remember that not all felt markers are waterproof! Test your medium carefully to make certain that it will not run when you block your work.

I prefer working with wool, but dollhouse rugs can be made with silk or cotton. All thread used for needlepoint must be colorfast. Make certain that whatever ply or weight you use covers the canvas completely while pulling through the holes with ease. The best way to determine the amount of thread you need is to work a square inch in the type of stitch and with the materials you are planning to use. You can then estimate the amount of thread needed by multiplying the amount used in the sample by the number of square inches in that particular color. Most needlepoint shops can estimate the amount of thread needed for a particular project with almost uncanny accuracy. Always make certain that you have enough thread for a particular project, as dye lots change and it is often impossible to match colors later.

When starting a project, allow at least a 2″ margin of plain canvas around the needlepoint design. Bind all the raw edges of the canvas with masking tape, double-fold bias tape or even adhesive tape. There are no set rules on where to begin a design. Many people prefer to start in the exact center, especially when working a centrally designed pattern, but others always start in a corner. Practice will tell you which method you prefer.

I recommend that you use the basketweave stitch whenever possible in making your dollhouse rugs. This stitch will not pull the canvas out of shape—an especially useful feature when working on small gauge canvas.

After you have finished stitching your miniature rug it must be cleaned and blocked. Soak it in cold water and Woolite until it is clean. Next, turn it upside down on a blocking board. Any hard, flat surface that you do not mind marring with nail holes and one that will not be warped by wet needlepoint can serve as a blocking board. Making sure the corners are straight, tack the canvas to the blocking board using *rustproof* tacks or staples through the unworked part of the canvas. When it is completely dry (after 24–48 hours), remove it from the board. It should remain rectangular; if it doesn't, dampen the needlepoint and repeat the blocking process. When you are certain that it is blocked correctly, steam the needlepoint with a steam iron to fluff up the wool. Make fringes for both ends using one or more of the pattern colors. Then either do a binding or whip stitch along the other two sides, leaving a strong, even edge. Steam the rough edges down so that the rug lies flat. On the bottom side secure both the fringe and the rough edges with a good white rabbit-skin glue. If you want to line the bottom, use a very thin fabric and catch-stitch it to the rug at the edges. Keep in mind that a lining will increase the thickness of your rug.

If there are any bits of white canvas showing through, dab a little paint on them. Your rugs are now ready to decorate your dollhouse and to enhance your miniature collections for years to come.

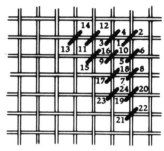

BASKETWEAVE STITCH: Start the basketweave in the top right-hand corner. Work the rows diagonally, first going down the canvas from left to right and then up the canvas from right to left. The rows must be alternated properly or a faint ridge will show where the pattern has been interrupted. Always stop working in the middle of a row rather than the end so that you will know in which direction you are working.

Miniature Needlepoint Rugs for Dollhouses

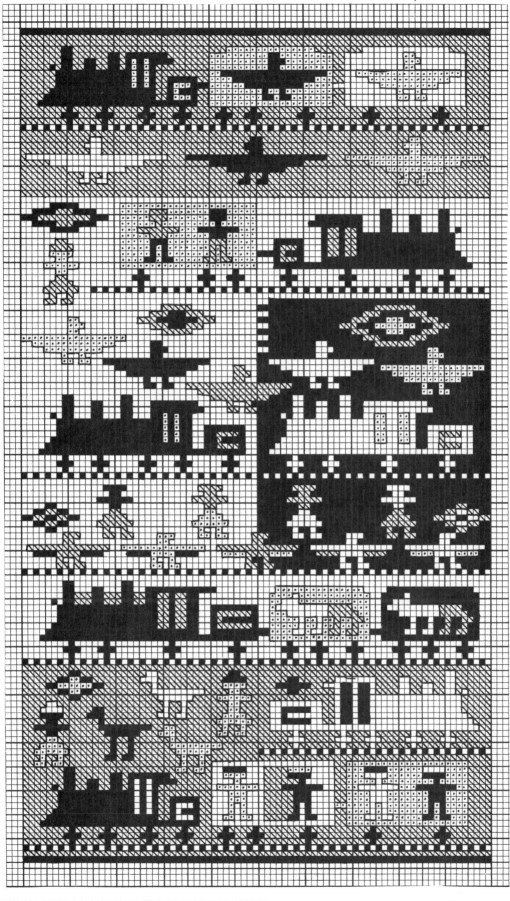

DESIGN FROM A NAVAJO "RAILROAD" BLANKET

■ navy blue
◨ red
⊡ grey
☐ white

MODERN NAVAJO RUG

2

DESIGN FROM AN 1870 NAVAJO SERAPE

■ brown
◨ ochre
☐ light gold

3

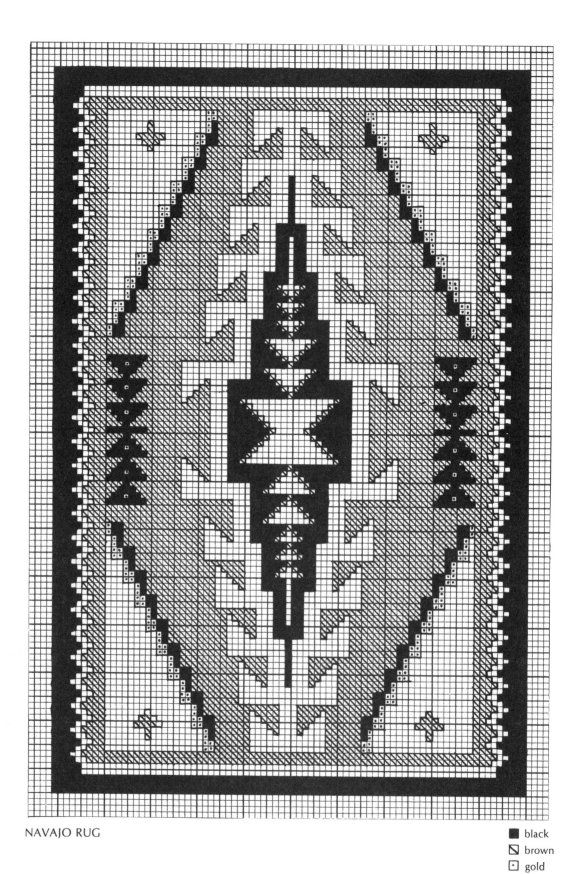

NAVAJO RUG

■ black
◩ brown
⊡ gold
□ white

4

"HOLBEIN" RUG. FROM HANS HOLBEIN'S PORTRAIT OF GEORGE GYSCZE

■ black
◪ red
⊡ gold
☐ white

5

ROMANIAN KILIM

■ black
◨ blue
⊡ red
☐ white

MONGOLIAN RUG

■ dark brown
☑ rust
⊡ ochre
☐ off-white

MODERN CHINESE RUG. Chart represents half of the rug; to complete
it, do the mirror image. *Do not repeat center line*

■ dark blue
⊡ medium blue
□ white

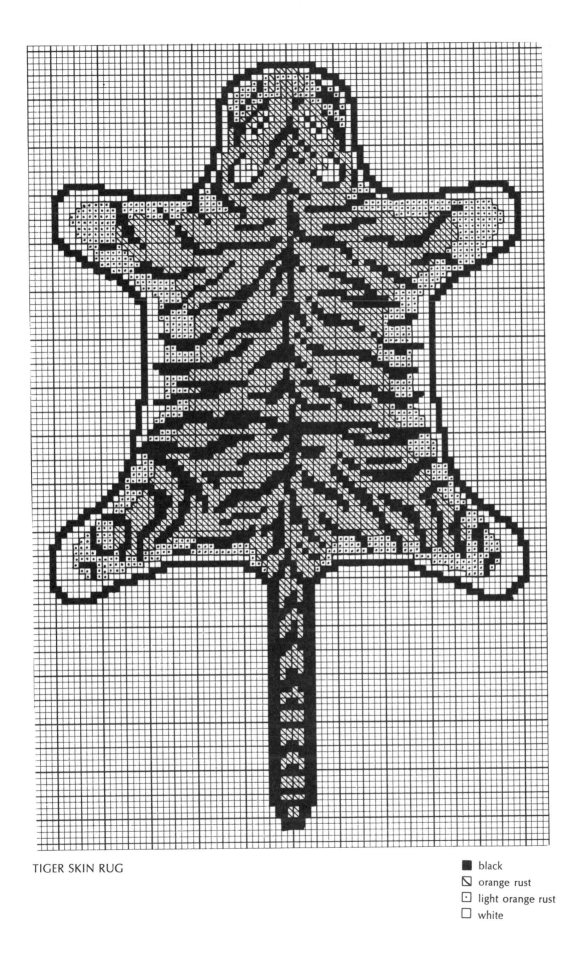

TIGER SKIN RUG

■ black
◩ orange rust
⊡ light orange rust
☐ white

Rendered in needlepoint on the cover

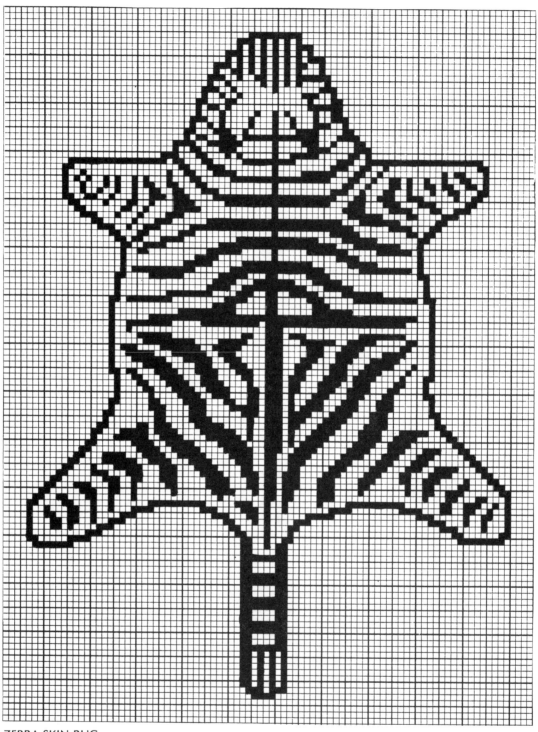

ZEBRA SKIN RUG

■ black
□ white

DINING ROOM CARPET

■ dark gold
◩ medium gold
□ pale gold

WELCOME MAT

■ dark brown
□ light brown

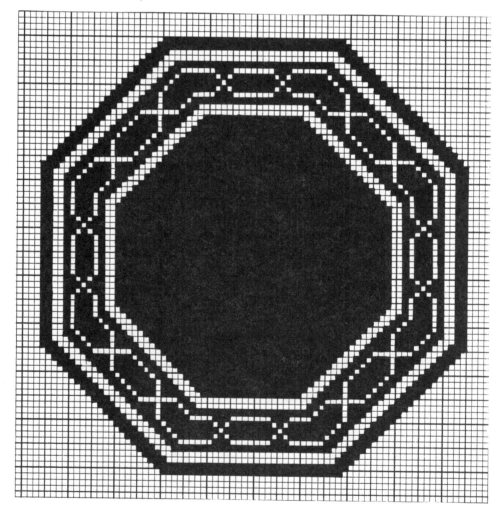

OCTAGONAL AREA RUG

■ solid color
□ white

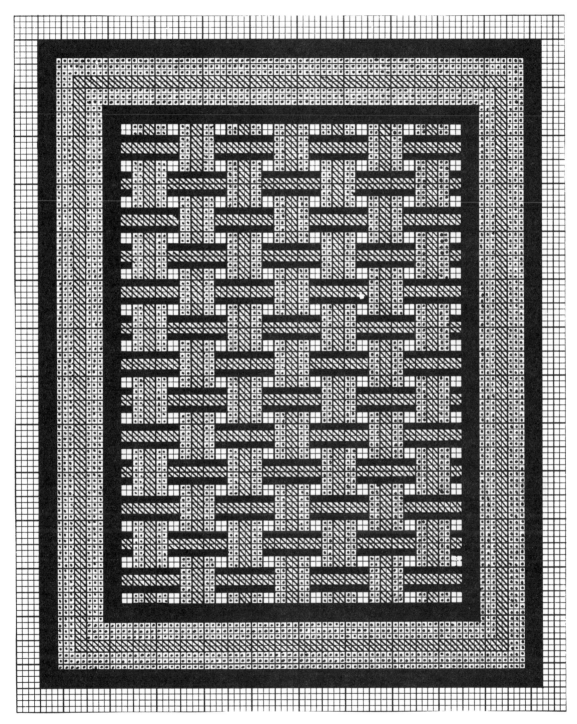

MODERN AREA RUG

- ■ dark green
- ⊡ gold
- □ ivory
- ☑ light green

MEDGEDIA GEORDEZ PRAYER RUG. See enlargement on
opposite page for color coding of central motifs

■ brown   ◧ pink
◪ red   ⊡ ochre
⊠ blue   ☐ pale gold
◹ brownish-green

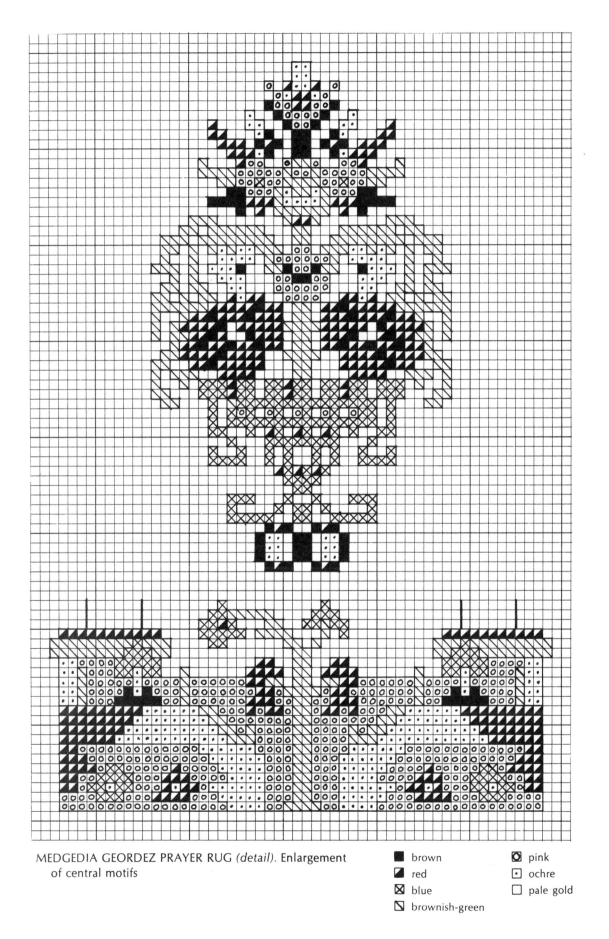

MEDGEDIA GEORDEZ PRAYER RUG *(detail)*. Enlargement
of central motifs

■ brown   ◨ pink

◪ red   · ochre

⊠ blue   ☐ pale gold

◩ brownish-green

KURDISH KILIM

■ dark brown	◨ orange-rust
◪ blue	⊡ ochre
◳ red	☐ ivory

DESIGN FROM A YAMONT BOKHARA TENT BAG

■ navy blue	⊡ pale gold
◪ deep red	□ off-white
◩ red	

HERIZ CARPET

■ navy blue	⊡ gold
◪ medium blue	☐ white
◩ red	

MUDJUR PRAYER RUG

■ purple ⊡ red
◪ rust ☐ gold
◩ green

MASLAGHAN RUG

■ black
◪ rust
◩ medium blue

⊡ ochre
□ pale gold

KARADJA RUNNER. Repeat motifs to
make runner the desired length

- ■ deep red
- ▨ medium blue
- ◩ red
- ⊡ ochre
- ☐ white

EARLY KUBA RUG

■ black   ⊡ och

◪ grey   ☐ wh

◳ red

22

GENJE RUNNER. Repeat motifs to
make runner the desired length

■ blue
◣ light blue
▨ red
⊡ yellow
☐ white

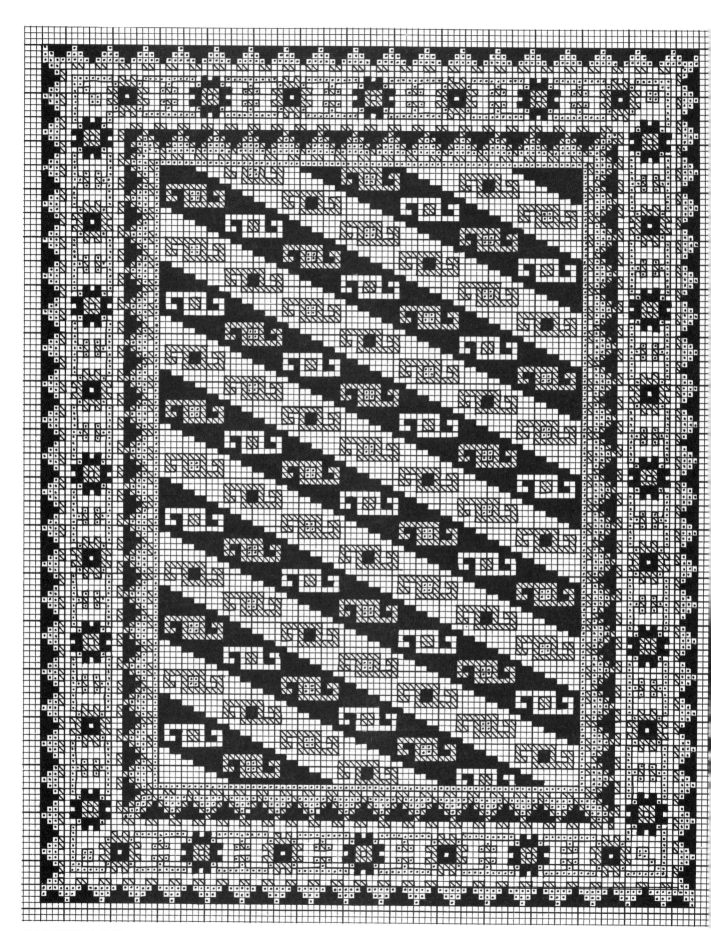

DAGHESTAN RUG

■ navy blue   ⊡ light blu[e]

◩ maroon   ☐ pale gol[d]

24

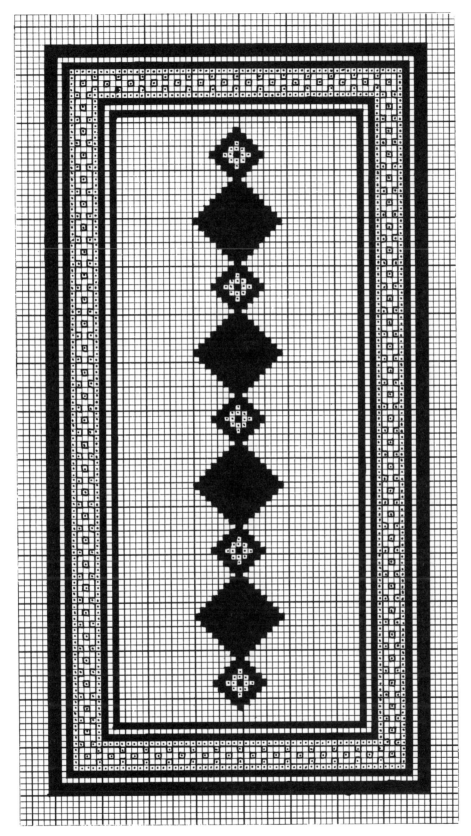

GEBBEH RUG

■ brown
□ ivory
⊡ tan

BALUCHI RUG

■ black
⊡ red
□ white
⊘ dark red

BALUCHI PRAYER RUG

1800 KAZAK RUG. See opposite page for detailed color coding

■ black	⊡ olive green
◪ blue	⊡ gold
⊠ rust	☐ white
◩ red	

28

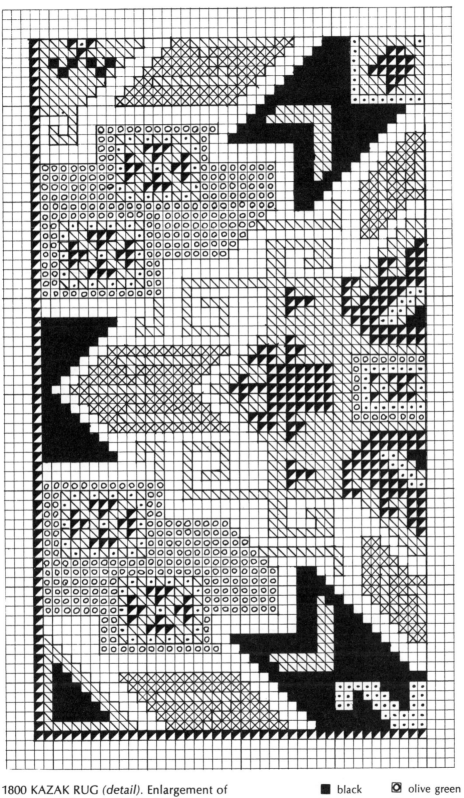

1800 KAZAK RUG *(detail)*. Enlargement of
bottom left quarter of design

■ black		◎ olive green	
◪ blue		⊡ gold	
⊠ rust		□ white	
◹ red			

SMALL KAZAK RUG

■ black
⊡ red — DMC 815
□ tan
▨ dark turquoise

GREEK RED TULIP RUG

	deep red		pink
	green		white
	deep gold		

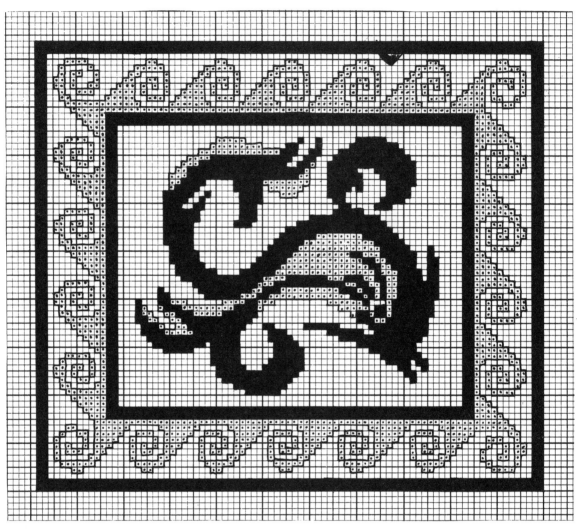

GREEK DOLPHIN RUG

■ dark blue
□ white
⊡ light blue

MODERN MOROCCAN RUG

■ brown   ⊡ orange
◣ red   □ white
◪ ochre

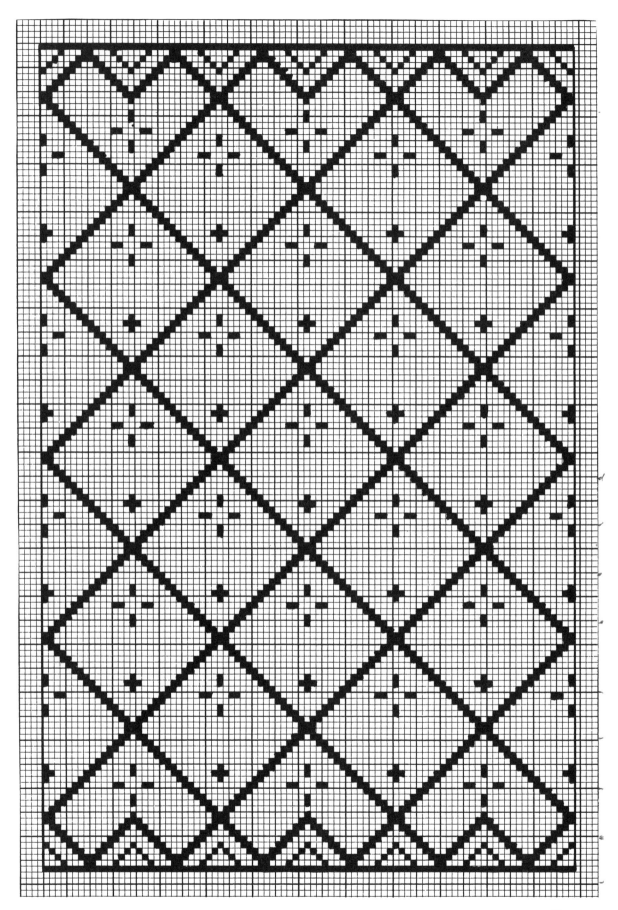

MODERN MOROCCAN RUG

■ brown
□ white

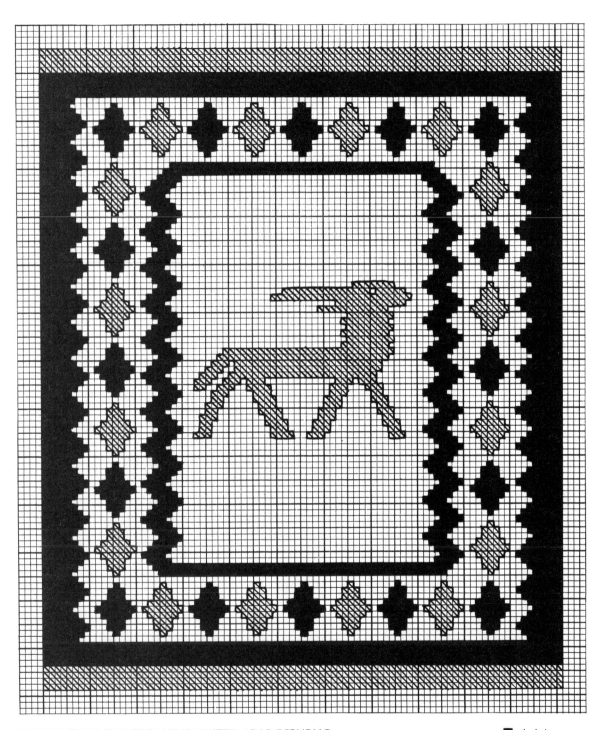

HANDWOVEN RUG FROM THE UNITED ARAB REPUBLIC

■ dark brown
◨ medium brown
□ off-white

EARLY AMERICAN HOOKED RUG. See enlargement on opposite page for color coding of central motif

■ dark brown	◙ light green
◩ dark green	⊡ yellow
⊠ red	☐ white
◪ dark gold	

36

EARLY AMERICAN HOOKED RUG *(detail)*.
Enlargement of half of central motif

■ dark brown		◨ light green
◪ dark green		⊡ yellow
⊠ red		☐ white
◻ dark gold		

PATRIOTIC AMERICAN RUG. See enlargement on opposite page for color coding of central motif

■ dark brown		◨ ochre	
⊠ blue		⊡ light ochre	
◪ red		☐ ivory	
◨ rust			

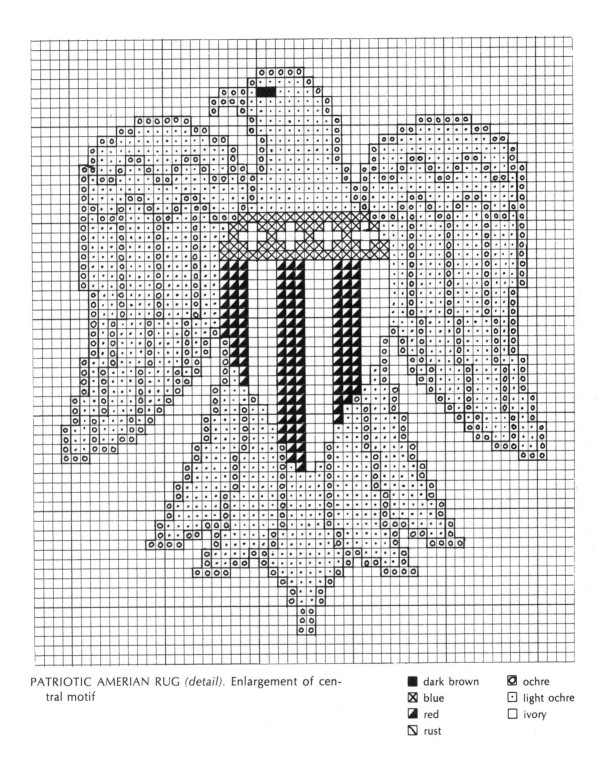

PATRIOTIC AMERIAN RUG *(detail)*. Enlargement of central motif

■ dark brown	◙ ochre
☒ blue	⊡ light ochre
◪ red	☐ ivory
◹ rust	

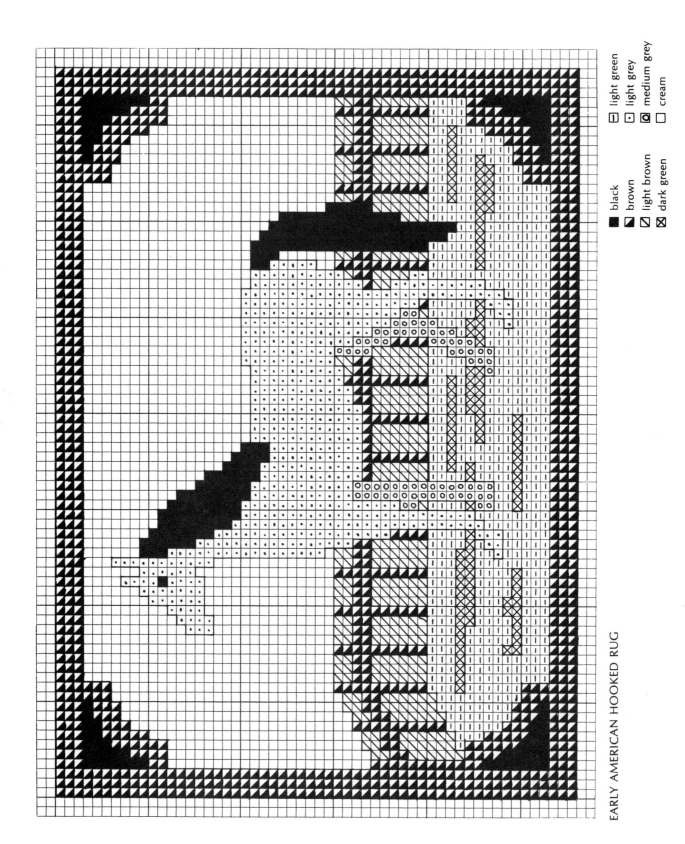

Legend:
- ■ black
- ◩ brown
- ◪ light brown
- ⊠ dark green
- ⊞ light green
- · light grey
- ◫ medium grey
- ☐ cream

EARLY AMERICAN HOOKED RUG

40